A New Age:
Problems & Potential

A NEW AGE: PROBLEMS & POTENTIAL

Kenneth R. Pelletier

ROBERT BRIGGS ASSOCIATES
SAN FRANCISCO

Published by
Robert Briggs Associates
Box 9
Mill Valley, California 94942

Project editor: Kathleen Goss
Designed by Mark Ong
First Broadside Edition 1985

ISBN# 0-931191-02-5

RBA: *This afternoon, in approaching the idea of the New Age—or A new age—and all of its problems and potential, one first has to realize that the New Age is the result of change, and one of the primary roots of that change has to be seen as the shift in scientific paradigm—that shift from strict determinism to uncertainty, brought on, of course, by quantum physics. Since this seems pretty well understood, perhaps it's best to try to get at how the implications of this shift have affected psychology and medicine, and ultimately the lives of concerned individuals everywhere.*

But first, perhaps, we need to say something about the dramatic rise in the importance of science itself. This has been a scientific century—from the first flight of the airplane in 1903 on, the list of technological miracles is dazzling. We all know it: wonder drugs, the atom bomb, television, space travel, nuclear energy, computers, robot manufacturing. The twentieth century, to say the least, has been historic. Yet even the casual observer of scientific disciplines knows that all is not well; the fanfare of the futurist might fall flat when one considers two grave problems. The first is the serious schisms. In science there is still a gap between leftover determinism and uncertainty. In medicine there is a schism between pathology and prevention, or holistic medicine. The most dramatic schism is in psychology between humanism and behaviorism, and, of course, in religion between the Eastern and Western traditions. The clash of East and West is especially felt in the United States.

The second problem is the growing absurdity of specialization. Let alone that the psychologist cannot understand the physicist, or the philosopher understand either of them, the fact is that specialization has become so extreme that, even within disciplines, specialists,

1

wedded to private and elaborate languages of specialization, cannot talk to each other. Now, what we'd like to address is the danger that these two problems could lead to deadly confusion. In the light of schisms and specialization, the question might be: who's minding the store? Who's attending to the crucial world view that society expects of these disciplines?

Pelletier: That was the the first question? That's a great one.

RBA: *Also, do these schisms contribute to specialization?*

Pelletier: To address that you need to go back in history. Since the late 1800s or early 1900s, there has been a literal explosion of information—in quantum physics, in biochemistry, in genetic engineering, in medicine, and in psychology. Partially in response to this overwhelming amount of new information, researchers began to shrink back from the really great problems, because it seemed as though any overreaching theory, or any generalization that someone could possibly reach, could be contradicted tomorrow—by a fact in a discipline in which you were not working, or by a new discovery that would happen in a year or two. The result of that seemed to be that scientists began tunneling in on smaller and smaller issues, which they felt could be refined and defined with more and more precision. There's a certain safety in precision because, in fact, you can know a great deal about something relatively small. That's security in the face of this overwhelming flood of information. In essence, this is the crisis predicted in 1960 in *The Structure of Scientific Revolutions* by Thomas Kuhn.

Unfortunately, that has not changed. There was a recent article that noted that there will be over 60,000 articles written in the general field of the neurosciences *this year*. Now, that's an utterly impossible amount of information for any person to absorb. So the tendency is to cull out of these 60,000 articles the 200 about which you know something, that are relevant to your field, so that you can feel competent, and know something about your particular area. The problem is that it leaves you a bit of an idiot savant. You're capable of performing an incredibly high-level, complex activity about relatively narrow and, perhaps, even unimportant information.

RBA: *Which do you think came first—the schisms or the specialization? Did one spawn the other?*

Pelletier: Hard to tell. At this point in time I think we're seeing the end of a crisis of the decline of religion and philosophy. In the Industrial Revolution—this would be the mid-1800s in Europe—

machines and technology. seemed to offer solutions that religion couldn't resolve. Religion was capable of addressing problems of ultimate value, need, and meaning, but it couldn't very well address problems of hunger, production of adequate foodstuffs, and clothing, and improving the physical standards of living—in other words, all the material enrichment that the Industrial Revolution made possible. So what seemed to have happened is that the breach, if you will, between ultimate religious-philosophical issues and more immediate human concerns about clothing, food, technology, and shelter seems to have widened. And—because as a species we tend to look at short-term gains and short-term goals—we have tended to be enamored of the products of science manifested through technology. We've become entranced by it. That's enhanced the schism. If you watch the progression from about the mid-1800s to the present, you find an enormous diminishment of concern about ultimate value—inner values—and a near fixation on wealth and material accumulation. This is not simply speaking in terms of the person who wants three cars—and one isn't enough—it's in the scientific realm as well. There's a wholesale preoccupation with only those things that can be seen or touched, defined or measured, in a very limited version of science that's not really the scientific method—it's really a scientific dogma.

RBA: *One of the things that concerns many people is the social fallout of all this, the repercussions on that lone individual out there who's educating himself or herself and is trying to live a larger, more positive life. And the one thing that comes to mind about this individual is the relationship between science and technology, or that very odd gulf between them. I think it can be said that the scientist creates technology, at least the means of technology, and scientific authority certainly authenticates technology. Nobody could say anything about nuclear energy when it was being introduced to the public because it was scientific. Yet, whenever science or the scientist is charged with the problems of technology, or the detrimental effects of technology, it seems that the answer is that technology is not science—that technology is only the use to which science is put. Science and/or the scientist is somehow divorced from responsibility. However, there never seems to be any technologist to blame for acid rain, nuclear waste, or fatal pesticides, and contemporary criticism of science or the scientist is seen as "an attack on science"—something that devoted scientists seem to regard as a sin equal to an attack on* *motherhood or God. Why do you think the relationship between science and technology is not more openly defined? In other words, if a scientist or any human being creates something new and, as a result, creates something that can or does threaten decent human existence, shouldn't that person accept responsibility?*

Pelletier: We need to remember that there are three levels in scientific endeavor. There's basic research, which may or may not have any practical applications whatsoever, which is simply pursued for the sake of answering a question, or attempting to answer a question. Then there is more applied science, more applied research, with a particular end point that you're trying to address. Will this artificial heart be a successful implant in a human being? That's a basic research question that would be explored with animals, with materials, but on a very limited level. Then the third level is really that of technology. That's when you go beyond the applied science area and into the realm of mass technology. You consider the production, and the potential mass production, of an artificial heart.

RBA: *Or nuclear energy.*

Pelletier: Or nuclear energy. So you need to see these three levels. The problem is that people confuse these levels. They think that a discovery in basic science will be isolated from its eventual technological manifestation or, conversely, that somehow the technological manifestation is consistent with the basic scientific insight. Like some of the basic inquiries into the nature of matter that gave rise to insights about the fundamental constituents of matter, of the universe. Certainly Einstein himself would never have condoned the development of nuclear weapons, nor the consequences of Hiroshima and Nagasaki. Yet the other dimension to this problem is that scientists are people, and bureaucracy is set up to diffuse responsibility. And scientists are inevitably and inextricably bound up in bureaucracy. They're in a laboratory, in a university, or working under private auspices; but they are always inextricably bound up within some form of bureaucracy. By its very nature, bureaucracy diffuses responsibility and diffuses authority. This makes ultimate accountability virtually impossible. This lack of responsibility and accountability spirals into the Union Carbide tragedy in Bhopal, Three Mile Island, Love Canal, or any toxic chemical exposure.

Now, to some degree the scientist has a legitimate stance in saying: I do not know to what end this research will be applied. Ultimately he or she cannot know what that end is going to be, so in that sense they're not responsible. But I do feel we have a moral obligation to oversee, to the best of our ability, the extent to which both basic and applied research are used, and ultimately to stay involved in the technological manifestations of research. This doesn't mean that at the end of that process that we must agree with each other. For instance, we have Edward Teller on one side of the issue of the development of nuclear weapons, and on the other we have Owen Chamberlain. These are two basic scientists who did not abdicate their responsibility, even though they have two totally different viewpoints.

RBA: *In other words, the scientist at the Lawrence Livermore Laboratory, who's not only in a bureaucracy but surrounded by hostile pickets, does have a responsibility as a human being to come out and engage—not necessarily to join, but engage—and evaluate the problem of the nuclear freeze.*

Pelletier: Yes, but there's absolutely no easy answer. You mention the Lawrence Livermore Laboratory. Actually I have conducted health promotion programs with the senior management at Lawrence Livermore for three years now, and I've been criticized by colleagues who say: you're just over there helping these people to be healthy enough to build better bombs that in fact are going to blow us all up! Now, that is a legitimate argument, and one that I've had to consider seriously, but it's different, as an abstract argument, from my experience, which is that there is an enormous range of difference among the fifty people I meet there every year. Some of them are hard-core militarists who would use whatever ability they have to develop weaponry, absolutely without question. Others have grave misgivings and interject conscience into their work—more conscience, I think, than many who would level criticism against the work they are doing. So, for me, it is not important that there's a global sanction for, or condemnation of, the use of nuclear weaponry. However, the responsibility remains, no matter on which side of the equation you fall, to act in accord with your own conscience, and to me the people at Lawrence Livermore are acting in accord with their conscience, to the best of their ability. I would rather have most of the men and women I've met inside—working on these developments—than outside, relatively powerless to influence the course, direction, and use of those technologies.

RBA: *Let's move on into the problem of the schism in psychology, between humanism and behaviorism. You might say that the implications of uncertainty on strict determinism have had a most dramatic effect on psychology. Some claim that recognition of these im-*

plications was indirectly responsible for ending the domination of Freudianism and behaviorism.

Pelletier: Well, again, the indeterminacy inherent in the Heisenberg Uncertainty Principle has been polarized. It's seen as either a great asset or a great liability, especially in psychological theory, in neurological theory, and questions about the brain/mind. On the negative side, Planck's constant is seen as a barrier to ever knowing the fundamental properties of the mind, because it places an absolute, ontological limit not just on the technology of measurement but on measurement per se. There is, as you know, a level below which quantum activity is no longer discernible, definable, measurable, quantifiable, or determinate. So this places an absolute limit on our ability to probe further into certain phenomena. Now, for those individuals in psychology or related areas who would like in fact to peg the absolute deterministic mechanisms of the nature of the mind, that is anathema. It's an anathema that had to be addressed approximately fifty years ago in physics by Niels Bohr, Wolfgang Pauli, and Werner Heisenberg. It's still being bandied about, but at least fifty years ago physics came to grips with this problem—eventually giving rise to Einstein's famous quip that "God does not play dice with the universe." Einstein was among those scientists who viewed uncertainty as an absolute anathema, because it interjected a lack of accountability, a lack of certainty, and it reduced the universe to operating on probability functions—in other words, not certainties but simply probabilities. And still, today, there are scientists in the neurosciences, and in psychology, who still see that as an anathema, because that ground is then forever incapable of being mapped.

On the other hand, another view is that this has been perhaps a great asset, and much is yet to be discovered about that. The rationale here is essentially that physics, as the master science, if you will—it's always been the vanguard of discovery—has finally and ultimately acknowledged a limit to physical observation of the nature of the universe. There's an often quoted statement by Sir James Jeans that the universe begins to look more "like a great thought than a great machine." And in that sense, you can see an opening. Here is the possibility of saying, yes, there are unquestionably mechanical, physical, atomic, and certainly quantum events that occur in physical matter and in the physical brain, but these are in fact not ultimately the constituents of what we refer to as mind or consciousness—that there is another level of reality, another level of observation that you cannot approach in the same way. So it leaves this other domain open to a different level, a different order of inquiry. An obvious example is that there are certain phenomena you can observe with a telescope, and they're not the same phenomena you can observe with a microscope, and no one would argue about one's superiority over the other. It depends on the nature of the events that you're measuring. So, when we have the Heisenberg Uncertainty Principle investing a certain level of subtle energy with non-observability, that leaves the avenue open to say: all right, what we have to do then is think of a different way of addressing that phenomenon. To me that's where the realm of consciousness, of mind-matter interaction, gets most exciting—when it's not ultimately reducible to the same parameters as the physical universe.

Actually, I discussed these issues in 1978 in *Toward a Science of Consciousness*. To me, the nature of the mind-body interaction is akin to the inextricable interaction between energy and matter. Again, from Wolfgang Pauli we have the principle of complementarity, which undercuts the supposed dualism of mind and brain, while preserving the status of each. In quantum physics the wave-versus-particle theory of light was resolved by postulating that these were *interchangeable* or complementary states. Whether a wave or a particle is observed is dependent on the experimental situation. Perhaps we have yet to discover the analogous complementarity of mind and brain.

RBA: *In the United States in the past twenty years, on one practical social level, what this seems to have translated into is the end of strict Freudian analysis. Certainly you don't see the degree or the domination of Freudian principles that you did in the 1950s. Has the effect of uncertainty on determinism been the cause of this?*

Pelletier: It has, yes, but there was a fatal flaw in psychoanalysis—more than one, but certainly at least *a* major fatal flaw— and it goes back to what we were talking about earlier, the difference between basic research and applied research. Freudian theory is basic research. Freud's inquiries into the nature of the mind, the stages of psychosexual development, represent one level of theoretical elegance about the nature and structure of the mind. The second level is its application in a very particular form of therapy called psychoanalysis. Those are two very, very different realms. Then you have a third level, which is the mass technology, if you will. These are the people—*not* the neo-Freudians—from the institutional training programs who then en masse practice the technology of psychoanalysis. These are three very, very different levels. You can criticize the shortcomings of psychoanalysis on any one of them. I think the theoretical underpinnings—Freud's basic theories about the nature and structure and functions of the mind—still have tremendous validity. As a footnote, they are also perhaps least understood. There are many individuals who now practice what they call psychoanalysis or psychotherapy who have, in fact, read very little of Freud, certainly have never read him in the German, with the nuances of the German language—how Freud saw the nature and function and structure of the mind. His vision is often very different from what it is interpreted as being.

RBA: *Which is the point of Bruno Bettelheim's recent book,* Freud and Man's Soul.

Pelletier: Exactly. I think Bettelheim's book is a major contribution to clarifying the fact of what the early Freud writings really meant— Freud *qua* Freud, not third-generation interpretations of Freud. But the second and more devastating argument is really in terms of its application. When in fact you develop theory in the late 1800s or early 1900s, in Victorian Vienna, you really have to raise the question of how relevant that becomes eighty years later, with a radically different culture, radically different problems—

RBA: *—in a different world—*

Pelletier: —in an entirely different world. So you had a model that essentially took five sessions a week, one hour in length, for five to seven years of time, in order to resolve early traumatic events and their consequences. That is completely untenable now. That model hardly even exists any more. The question that comes up is: how applicable is psychoanalysis outside of that cultural context or pre-scribed methodology? In other words, can you do it once a week for two years, or once a week for a month? I really have some grave misgivings and doubts about that form of application. A second point is that the recognition of the unconscious, the discovery of the deeper substrates of the mind by Freud, came at a time of Surrealist painting. It came at a time of further appreciation of Mesmerism, hypnosis, Salvador Dali, then James Joyce, and Carl Jung. It came at a time when these insights into the unseen, unstructured nature of the mind were absolutely flourishing. There was a general cultural preoc-cupation with the act of discovery and information about the nature of the mind.

On the negative side, there was an inordinate preoccupation with the darker side of the unconscious—a realm of suppression, repression, denied sexuality, murderous and incestuous impulses —essentially a subterranean, seething cesspool. Unfortunately, this emphasis completely ignored the higher dimensions of human consciousness evident in Jung's collective archetypes, Maslow's peak experiences, or in the vast Eastern literature concerning the attainment of samadhi and enlightenment, especially in the Zen and Tibetan Buddhist practices, which are over 2,000 years old. Not only do these provide insight into the unconscious and superconscious, but they precisely describe practices—an "inner science" for the Tibetans—that constitute an inner technology for the transformation of human consciousness.

What has changed at present is that while those basic discoveries remain, what kind of practical application—efficacious for real people living in a real world—comes out of them? That's where you begin to get more behavioral approaches—a behavioral technology of change that is more direct, less contingent on insight, and, in fact, produces a much greater and relatively permanent change in a shorter period of time. Those approaches have tended to dwarf, just by outcome and efficacy, the basic applications of psychoanalysis.

RBA: *Coming back to Freud, just as an interesting aside, he's recently been attacked about his reversal of theory attributing neurosis in adults to sexual seduction in childhood. It's said Freud changed his mind and reported that childhood molestations were not fact but fantasy. This has been sensationalized by some critics; however, other more sober investigators have made the same point. Karl Menninger is quoted as once saying, "Why, oh, why, couldn't Freud believe his own ears?" Do you think Freud reversed himself and, if so, why?*

Pelletier: It's clear, at least from Jeffrey Masson's *The Assault on Truth*—if the documentation is accurate—that Freud did reverse his position in 1905, and publicly retracted the seduction theory. He did in fact begin to entertain the sexual seduction of children and molestation of children as a pure fantasy, something to be analyzed rather than taken seriously and the real situation corrected. Therefore he did reverse himself and began to think of it as a fantasy rather than as an actual occurrence. Particularly in light of present concerns over child abuse, this stance actually retarded the recognition of the sexual, emotional, and physical trauma of incest and child abuse in both psychoanalysis and psychotherapy as a whole.

RBA: *But critics charge he did this because his original theory was so violently attacked by the medical establishment when he first presented it in Vienna.*

Pelletier: Well, I think that was probably true. Again it goes back to the fact that if you are a pioneer, if you're essentially a physician—there was no such thing as psychiatry then—if you're in Vienna and you are telling people that fathers are molesting their children and mothers are fondling their sons—well, to say the least, this raises mayhem even now. In this past year we've had an explosion of recognition of child abuse and how awfully traumatic it is. Take that back eighty or ninety years and place it in a much more conservative society, turn-of-the-century Victorian Vienna, and you can understand how anyone, even Freud, suffered. The peer pressure on him to not lift the lid, not uncover this social reality, but simply to reduce it to a fantasy to be analyzed, would be absolutely staggering! So it's not all that surprising that anyone would essentially reverse a public statement that would fly in the face not only of professional colleagues, but the whole Viennese or world society.

Finally, one last point I would like to make is that I find the entire overemphasis and preoccupation with psychoanalysis, not Freud per se, to be anachronistic and a bit ridiculous. There are discoveries and ideas of infinitely greater importance to contemporary research and clinical practice in the realm of human consciousness. Clearly, the monumental genius of Jung remains underestimated; the genius of Sherrington, Pavlov, Cannon, Skinner, Penfield, Selye, Sperry, and Eccles, and the contributions of quantum physicists—Priogogine, and the holographic models of the brain by Bohm and Pribram—these are all of infinitely greater importance in resolving contemporary issues of the nature of mind-body interaction. Psychoanalysis has been an invaluable step, but to reify one contribution among many is really much ado about nothing.

RBA: *Perhaps, but for the sake of our afternoon, let's talk a bit about the division of the brain, about which I know you have some things to say. Recently, a great deal of emphasis has been put on the right brain/left brain differentiation. Is it as important as some people claim? In other words, might I break through somehow and develop my right brain and change my life into one peak experience?*

Pelletier: The claims made for left and right brain research remind me of Mark Twain's statement, "The reports of my death are greatly exaggerated," because that is in fact the case. There are well-documented attributes, noted in the 1860s by neurologist John Hewlings

10

Jackson, and characteristics of each half of the cortex of the brain—the left hemisphere being essentially analytical, sequential, temporal, rational, and linguistic, with the right hemisphere being more field/ground, gestalt, musical, spatial, more involved in the recognition of faces and emotions, and essentially the part of the brain that recognizes the forest, whereas the left side of the brain recognizes the specific trees. And the distinction does hold true, but even that distinction is based largely on studies with right-handed males who tend to be the most asymmetrical—who tend to have these functions most asymmetrically distributed in the brain.

RBA: *A left-handed male would say amen to that.*

Pelletier: A left-handed male has them less symmetrically distributed, and a right-handed female even less than either of the two males. A left-handed female essentially has functions almost symmetrically distributed. Generally, the two hemispheres of the female brain are more connected and in harmony than in that of men. So yes, there's a kernel of truth, there's unquestionably a reality to the fact that these functions are divided into areas of the brain. There are several evolutionary theories, such as that of Julian Jaynes, about how this has occurred. The reality is that none of us would sacrifice one hand because we preferred our right to our left. When you listen to the proponents of enhancing the right-hemisphere experience or enhancing the left-hemisphere experience—the left-hemisphere experience would be the superlearning approach—or adulation of right-hemisphere function—the artistic or mystical experience, or the kind of "aha!" recognition more characteristic of right-hemisphere function—you find it all completely inappropriate.

The reality is that the brain acts in concert. It trades off. There's a waxing and waning to the electrical activity of the brain. There's a waxing and waning to the information that it shares. Moreover, what's overlooked is that the largest bundle of nerves in the brain, the corpus callosun, *connects* the two hemispheres.

Now, according to the newest DNA research by Sibley and Ahlquist, the brain has been designed over the course of seven million years of evolution to function with the two halves *in concert*. Why else would evolution develop such an enormous nerve connection? The point is that the brain is really designed to function as an intact, ongoing, holographic organ.

One last point on that is—again, much like the deterministic, limited versions of science—there's always been, throughout history, an attempt to isolate certain very specific functions of the brain in very localized regions of the brain. Phrenology was an obvious attempt. Lumps on the head were supposed to tell you something about what went on in the person's brain. Most superficial approaches have been wonderfully dismissed in Stephen Jay Gould's *The Mismeasure of Man*. We do know now that certain functions are more localized. There are certain areas of the brain that control, say, fine motor movement, speech, vision, and similar functions. But the more modern look at the brain is that although it's specialized in a particular area, the intact brain functions like a hologram where functions are inherent in each cell of the brain, although certain anatomical areas emphasize certain functions while other potentials remain dormant in those same areas. In other words, it's a very plastic organ for the human being, and this division of left/right is valuable, but excessive when it becomes dichotomania. The most important thing is to look at the brain intact, and appreciate its extraordinary design and function.

RBA: *One secondary question: is there a difference between the male and female brain?*

Pelletier: Oh, yes. Probably the one finding that emerges from the research is that there are sexual differences in the brain, and that the brain develops very differently, from immediately postpartum throughout the life, for men and for women. There are physical differences in male and female brains in the corpus callosum, the hypothalamus, and the amygdala. There is clear evidence from the research of Marian Diamond at Berkeley that, at least in animals, the right hemisphere of the male is thicker, and the left of the female. This is largely based on experiments manipulating hormones, to "masculinize" female animals in their sexual and aggressive behavior with testosterone, and "feminize" male animals with estrogen into behavior such as male birds singing the female songs of their species. With all this, however, there are few clear *physiological* differences between male and female brains, but these hormonal manipulations clearly emphasize *behavioral, sexual,* and *aggressive* differences, based on masculinized or feminized brains.

Interestingly enough, for humans there tends to be a much greater use of the left hemisphere by women and of the right hemisphere by men, which contradicts our social stereotypes. Much of this is seen in Jerre Levy's pioneering work at the University of Chicago. There's superior acquisition of language and written words by women, and yet there's a better use of poetry, mathematics, and manipulation of three-dimensional objects by males. These do seem to be sexually determined differences in brain physiology and function. However, an even more important area is that various illnesses, both physical and psychological, tend to be different among men and women, and between left and right handers. These are due to hormonal changes—not just neurological changes, but hormonal changes—in the male and female brain. So out of all of this research, one of the most significant areas is probably the fact that there are inherent biological, genetically programmed, sexual differences in the human brain, and that these may have dramatic effects on health.

This is where things get really interesting. There is research by Norman Geschwind at Harvard that has found that left-handed people, governed predominantly by the right hemisphere, exhibit more dyslexia, migraine headaches, and autoimmune diseases such as myasthenia gravis (which afflicted Aristotle Onassis). Other research by Gerard Renoux of the medical school at Tours in France has discovered that the destruction of the left hemisphere in animals depresses the immune system, while destruction of the right seems to enhance it. It appears again that the left and right hemispheres work intact and *in concert,* with direct control by the left and modulation by the right. All of these findings are new and need to be sorted out, but the point is that the simplistic and reductionistic models of the left and right hemispheres are inadequate and the real insights and discoveries lie before us.

RBA: *This brings us to a big problem—the brain/mind problem. With the claims of behaviorists and neurobiologists, and the counter-claims of those more oriented to religion or mysticism, the controversy as to whether or not the mind is or is not contained in the brain continues to grow. As a matter of fact it seems to be becoming almost the intellectual Armageddon of the twentieth century. What do you think? Is the mind separate or outside of the brain, and if so, how?*

Pelletier: Boy, what a loaded question. Let me hedge, in a way—

RBA: *—before you do, we should note that the question comes from a previous conversation in which you mentioned that consciousness is to the mind what time is to the clock—if that's any help.*

Pelletier: That's exactly the way I wanted to *not* hedge the question, but, perhaps, address a different question. Look at it this way: when we set up a dichotomy between something that is not physical, meaning the mind, and something that we consider is physical, meaning the brain, and we then muse about whether the mind is inside or outside the brain, that's totally anachronistic —an out-of-date model that has nothing to do with what we now know about inert matter, much less biological matter. My point is that it is simply the wrong question. A more appropriate one is the same question we ask about the nature of the relationship between any subtle energy and any supposedly inorganic and inert matter, which is: how do they interact? We've already mentioned my favorite analogy about how time is not *in* the watch. It's true, however, that time without the watch is simply an abstract phenomenon that doesn't help us very much in day-to-day activities. The watch without a concept of time is simply a collection of gears that you could assemble in any way whatsoever. The point is, there's an interaction between the two.

I'm certain now, that in this decade, because of research in quantum physics, biochemistry, holographic models of the brain, in the areas of psychoneuroimmunology and psychology, in the advances in psychophysiology and the neurosciences, we will have a model—a basic model and an applied model—that will unequivocally demonstrate the interaction between a subtle energy we will be able to quantify and call mind, and the quantum energy levels of what we call the human central nervous system, or the brain. We will find that these are inextricable, and *ultimately not reducible one to the other*. I also believe that the methods of observation may not be by physical instrumentation. Now, physicists already have an acknowledged level—essentially the Heisenberg Uncertainty Principle—that makes it ontologically impossible to measure certain phenomena. You can infer what phenomena might be, but you cannot measure them directly. We are going to have precisely the same kind of circumstance in the neurosciences, where we will infer certain properties of consciousness from observing the subtle level of energy in the brain, central nervous system, and biochemistry, but none will be reducible to the others. The attempt is always either to reduce mind to some field flux at the quantum level or to some biochemical agitation; or in the absence of that, to say, well, if we cannot reduce it to these measures—very crude, by the way—then in fact it must be outside of the brain. Yet there is no support for such an assumption. It simply means that we are presently incapable of theorizing elegantly enough to uncover what the nature of this interaction is. It doesn't mean that it does not exist. What we need is a complementarity principle of human consciousness.

RBA: *One thing that comes to mind here is some of the interesting work that seems to be coming out of past life therapy. Many claims are obviously bogus, yet often when a therapist deals with deeper patterns of memory—not simply the patterns of this life but the patterns of remembered lives—it seems to be more successful in righting wrongs or dissolving the neurosis—more so than had the therapy concentrated on the present life. Now, wouldn't one need to transcend the material brain and enter an ethereal mind in order to go back into the memory of past lives?*

Pelletier: You really want me to walk on thin ice, don't you!

RBA: *Let's ask something else. Have you seen what you would consider any meaningful work going on in past life therapy? The key to this seems to be the range of memory. There seem to be many cases where past life therapy succeeds where current traditional therapy fails. This seems to be true with problems of sexual identity.*

Pelletier: Again, just as we've been discussing all afternoon, our perceptions of certain problems, and therefore the questions we come up with, are colored by historical precedents, both positive and negative. As soon as we say the words "past life," it's negative. Certainly in modern Western science, it's immediately negative. It's not scientific. So anything you say after that is nonsense, okay? If I say, yes, I've seen significant work done in "past life" therapy, it's immediately dismissed, because we have certain associations with those words, those concepts. Regardless of the fact that about three-fourths, if not more, of the world population's religions in fact believe in such a reality.

By the way, the Dalai Lama has pointed out that the Western mind has great difficulty in accepting the sequencing of multiple lives suggested by reincarnation. He went one better and indicated that multiple lifetimes do not occur in sequence but *simultaneously.* His analogy was that of a telephone transmission that carried hundreds of conversations simultaneously but slightly out of phase in space and time. In any case, this is an enormous and complex subject that is not clearly understood and therefore reduced to simplistic concepts or straw-man dismissals.

But let me address this in a different way. Even if it is a fantasy that a person experiences, which we in turn label past life—the person sees himself as an Egyptian overseer who brutalizes slave building pyramids and therefore in this life is suffering from low back pain because of the weight he had made others carry—now, under hypnotic regression, with use of visualization or fantasy, it's not at all uncommon for people to begin to report these kinds of occurrences. That's a fairly frequent—in fact a very frequent—phenomenon. (This occurred during my clinical work with Gregory Bateson, when we used such approaches during his treatment for an inoperable malignancy in his right lung.) The fact that this can help to resolve a neurosis, psychosis, or even a physical, organic problem in this lifetime is well documented. Even the regression of ostensibly terminal diseases, as reported in the classic *Spontaneous Remission of Cancer* by Everson and Cole, and, in numerous case studies, the regeneration of deteriorated organs is documented. One surprising source is a series of over sixty stringently investigated medical "miracles" researched by highly qualified medical teams, which I read on file at Lourdes, France. Virtually all such cures or spontaneous remissions involved intense, emotionally charged memories and images, which were on occasion of different periods in history.

So the key question is: was this a "real experience"? In other words, was this really an historically accurate record of the person's life at some point hundreds of years ago? I don't think we know one way or the other. In fact, very often the person doesn't even care. What they care about is the fact that they are no longer anxious, or their physical symptom is gone. On the other hand, another person may become totally infatuated with such mental phenomena and want to get more and more "life readings." They become addicted. They want to go to a psychic or a guru and hear who they were, or they want to have ten readings to be sure they know all hundred people that they've been, what they've done, and all the occurrences. That to me is equally neurotic. For me the touchstone is, does this therapy produce efficacy for the person in their life, right here, right now? On another level, what the community thinks about how we then label that outcome is a whole other matter. A community in Tibet views the "reality" of the "past life" experience in an obviously different light than a community in Boston. Most people come into treatment, or therapy, because they're interested in helping themselves function better—right now.

RBA: *Results, yes. One other thing that is interesting is that most serious past life therapists do not advertise what they do. They seem to want to keep a low profile to avoid needless sensationalism.*

Another question seems relevant at this point. You started out at the beginning talking about the change in the scientific model, and how we're limited by uncertainty to possibly not being able to observe phenomena, or not being able to describe them. It seems that what's emerging with a lot of the things we've been talking about is a new scientific model that is actually a very old scientific model, which we could call a "black box" model. In this model we can define what's put in and what comes out, yet we have no idea what's inside. At times we don't seem to care, whereas the old scientific model focused on what was inside the black box, and if you couldn't describe what the processes were and explain what was going on, then it wasn't good science. Today it seems as if, in many of the areas we've been talking about, we're becoming much more empirical in the way that we're doing science or doing therapy. As long as results are what we're looking for, as long as we know what we need to do to get those results, it doesn't matter what the explanation is.

Pelletier: Yes and no. It depends on how big you draw the black box. The Heisenberg Uncertainty Principle is an infinitesimally small black box and, quite literally, it means simply that you cannot determine both the position and the momentum of a fundamental particle at the same time. This infinitesimal uncertainty is Planck's constant, or -6.77×10^{-27}. That's really all that it says, so that we have an infinitesimally small black box. And we have not even come close to pressing to that limit in terms of the nature of the interaction between subtle energy and gross matter in the human brain. So my position is that we need to push much further before we invoke this concept of the black box. The interior interaction between mind and matter, mind and brain, is now unobservable, unknown, *terra incognita*, but I'm not willing to throw up my hands and say that's right—that we have to draw these boundaries very, very large, very indeterminately and prematurely—because we haven't even begun to approximate the quantum level at which these subtle energy interactions must occur.

Let me say a bit more about possible models of the brain. Roger Sperry, the Nobel Prize winner in medicine two years ago, made some important points. Sperry is the psychologist who formulated the original hypotheses about the split brain, having tested a patient who had the corpus callosum severed for intractable epilepsy by the neurosurgeon Joseph Bogen in the early 1950s. Sperry has subsequently made a fascinating series of statements. You would think that here is a scientist who spent his life in what reductionists would see as an attempt to reduce mind and consciousness to the fundamental material properties of the brain, when in fact his recent articles and his statements when he accepted the Nobel Prize would indicate quite the opposite. And— I like the company—he's much more akin to this interactionist model we are discussing. He stated three hypotheses quite explicitly. One is that at a certain level of development—which as yet remains undefined—at a certain embryonic level of development, there is a property that arises out of the critical mass of brain cells that is consciousness; it is the rudimentary form— undifferentiated, not anything that we would call fully developed consciousness; but this consciousness now emerges out of this critical mass of cells. This is akin to the concept of critical mass in physics, chemistry, or biology. Secondly, this critical mass then begins to exert a "superordinate" influence over the further differentiation and development of this biological mass. So it then exerts, in Sperry's words, "a superordinate downward influence"; or it will literally govern how this mass then develops into what we call the human brain. The third property, which is even more fascinating, is that once this superordinate mind or property of consciousness has emerged, it is at that point irreducible; from that point on it is forever irreducible to the fundamental material, biological tissues from which it arose.

One of Sperry's statements is so striking to me that I have committed it to memory. He describes his model of human consciousness as a "scheme that puts mind back over matter, not under or outside or beside it. It is a scheme that idealizes ideas and ideals over physical and chemical interactions, nerve impulse traffic, and DNA. It is a brain model in which conscious, mental, psychic forces are recognized to be the crowning achievement of some 500 million years or more of evolution." That nearly moves me to tears!

Now, Sperry's three hypotheses are really quite extraordinary, because he's not taking the dogmatic, reductionistic position that mind is reducible to mere chemistry and physics. He's absolutely not in that camp, and yet he's not in the other camp, which was perhaps more characteristic of Sir John Eccles, who has stated absolutely that mind is in fact independent, outside of the brain. In a 1984 interview in *U.S. News and World Report,* Eccles described his belief in a "mental spiritual world," and said that the claim by science that it can explain consciousness in terms of brain function was a modern *"superstition"*! I don't even think Eccles would really acknowledge an interaction, if you will, whereas Sperry is somewhere in the middle, tending toward the separation of brain and mind. But to me that was very significant and suggestive of what this new model might be like.

RBA: *Also suggestive of the path Wilder Penfield trod a generation or so before.*

Pelletier: Absolutely. There's another example—Penfield's book, *Mystery of the Mind.* When Wilder Penfield, clearly one of the most eminent neurosurgeons of our time, was mapping the brain by electrical stimulation, he was dealing with the problem we referred to earlier: how localized in the physical brain are properties of consciousness? That was one of the reasons why he began to conduct the electrical stimulation of the unanesthetized brain. One particular occurrence he recounts in *Mystery of the Mind* was that when he stimulated the left sensorimotor region, which controls fine motor movement on contralateral sides of the body, the man on the operating table flexed his right index finger. Penfield asked, did that feel like it does when you move your finger? The man said no, it felt as though someone reached over and pressed my finger and moved it for me. This incident produced a significant insight for Penfield, which is: by electrical stimulation you can produce sham motor movement, but this is not the same, subjectively, as voluntary movement of the finger. Now again this is a very subtle differentiation between the electrical activity of the brain and conscious volition, but nonetheless that's the area where the breakthroughs will happen.

RBA: *Before we move on into medicine and have you talk about psychoneuroimmunology, on which we want to spend time, we want to touch upon the problem of narcissism, which, as a criticism of the New Age, seems to have become an industry in itself. The human potential movement does concentrate on the self and above all, on self-improvement. Yet it's recognized that that borders on narcissism, which, to be sure, can be a negative, destructive condition. But when does positive concern for the self become narcissistic? And would you agree with critics of the human potential movement such as Christopher Lasch, who maintain that the whole human potential movement is crippled by narcissism?*

Pelletier: Narcissism again is a word that is misused. Yes, there are aspects of narcissism in the New Age culture. You can point out a preoccupation with self—a preoccupation with just the right diet, just the perfect amount of exercise, a certain hair style, or contemporary clothing—

RBA: *—or a certain guru—*

Pelletier: —a certain guru. There's no question that there is an element of narcissism in our contemporary culture as a whole—it's not limited to the human potential movement. On the other hand, to confuse that self-indulgent narcissism with serious inquiry into the nature of the mind is to have totally missed the point. Recently, in November, along with twenty others, I was invited to a conference at Amherst College in Massachusetts to meet for five days with the fourteenth Dalai Lama. The purpose was for the Dalai Lama to lecture and for the scientists to respond, to see if it was possible to translate the insights of Tibetan Buddhism into contemporary psychological and neurophysiological theory. Someone who sees narcissism everywhere—rather like: "If it walks like a duck, talks like a duck, it must be a duck"—could easily have dismissed this entire conference as a gross exercise in narcissism, because of all that this man talked about. All that the 2,500 years of his spiritual tradition and meditation focused on was self-exploration and the disciplined focusing of the human mind. His essays, published in a 1984 anthology, *Kindness, Clarity, and Insight,* contain the essence of this Buddhist "middle way."

The point being—and this emerged very strongly at the conference—there is one fundamental tenet: until you know yourself, all of your actions proceed in error, and actions that proceed in error lead to disaster both for the self and the greater collective society. So, actually, the lone individual you mentioned before has an absolute responsibility to know her or his motivations—to know who they are, to know why they are doing what they are doing, to bring the greatest possible clarity they can to the actions that they undertake in the world. And no one can abdicate this responsibility. The more responsibility a person has in the physical world—if they're a general in the Pentagon, if they're the head of a major corporation, if they're a religious leader in the modern world, be it the Pope, the Dalai Lama, or an American Indian—they have an even greater responsibility to ensure that whatever actions they take proceed out of clarity of mind. Now to me that has absolutely no relationship to the rather superficial aspects of narcissism that should be justifiably dismissed—right now—in our culture.

RBA: *Let's touch just a minute on this. If the human potential movement grew out of the implications of uncertainty for determinism, it seems there is always a danger that the human potential* *movement itself will become somewhat deterministic. For instance, hasn't concern for the self, even when it's not narcissistic, become a flagrant looking-out-for-number-one, a trend that would have little or no therapeutic effect on the whole community of men and women? Because, after all, the real problem is the problem of psychological as well as physiological well-being. Perhaps psychophysiological well-being is what we're talking about? And such well-being has to include a social consciousness.*

Pelletier: Absolutely. If you take two of the most ancient traditions that advocate inner knowledge, the Tibetan and the Zen traditions of Buddhism, they are very clear, they are very scientific. The article in *The New York Times* about the conference was explicit about the fact that this was an investigation of "inner science"; in fact, that's precisely what the Tibetans term their meditative practices. They don't talk about escapism, self-involvement, or mysticism per se. They concentrate on a disciplined, precise inner science. You undertake certain procedures—you meditate, sit, breathe, work, look, visualize, and think in certain ways, which have highly predictable outcomes, replicable over time among different observers who follow the same procedures for measuring and observing the subsequent phenomena. The subsequent states of consciousness are defined in precise properties in the text of the *Abhidharma*—it is equivalent to the periodic table of the elements, but these are inner, psychological properties rather than material, chemical ones.

This is science in the strictest sense of the word. It simply happens to be an inner science rather than an outer science, which is what we Westerners have perfected. The Dalai Lama was asked during a public presentation why it was that he saw himself here, now, in the Western world? He said it was for a particular reason—that without the outer science people are impoverished. They don't eat well, they don't live well, they don't have adequate medical care, they don't have adequate housing. But without the inner science the meaning behind such a highly developed, materially richer existence is lost. So until we have an interaction between the inner and the outer technologies, we're lost. They need each other.

One last point is that in both Tibetan and Zen traditions, there is always, *always* a fundamental admonishment—which is that after you meditate, you go and cook your meal, sweep the yard, clean the bathroom, you go out and in fact are mandated to do social good—feed the poor, clothe the unclothed. In other words, there is an inseparable dimension of social-cultural service involved in the outward expression of whatever inner clarity a person attains. Again, that is vastly far removed from the absurd narcissism that is obviously self-indulgent in the strictest sense of Narcissus.

RBA: *Getting back to our lone, concerned individual out in a New Age—still beset with pain and pressures. Isn't the greatest problem still stress? Could you touch upon this? It's been suggested that exercise alone will not solve the problem of stress, and that in order to properly deal with total psychophysiological well-being, the concerned individual needs to control not only her or his consumption and exercise, but to develop a third, separate area of stress relaxation, such as meditation, in order to truly deal with the whole problem of stress. What are your thoughts about that?*

Pelletier: Categorically, *no one thing or practice*, no matter what it is, will resolve the problem of stress and optimal health. Exercise will not do it. Meditation or relaxation exercises per se will not do it. Diet will not do it. Making sure that you're not exposed to any toxic substances in your home or your workplace or your total planetary environment will not do it. Again, single-factor causation is an anachronistic residual from the old model of Newtonian physics—that this particular cause has a single effect, and only that cause has only that effect. Our thinking, if not the actual conduct of science, is riddled with this kind of misconception, and health, medicine, and psychology are where it becomes most obvious, and also most inadequate.

The point is that what I see as a problem, if you will, in a person who comes in and sees me on a clinical basis, is the product of a certain genetic history, a particular physical and medical history, a familial upbringing, a certain nutritional status, a level of stress, a work environment in which they're embedded, a set of spiritual concerns, and the social context in which they live. Now, for any given person at any given time, *one* of those areas is going to be the most important. For any person who has not excercised, exercise is going to be extremely important. For someone who's eating a poor, inadequate diet—even by the conservative U.S. Government dietary guidelines formulated by the McGovern Committee in 1977—that's obviously the single most important thing that they should be doing. But in our work, in our Behavioral Medicine Program in Internal Medicine at the University of California School of Medicine in San Francisco, the point is that we always urge the individual that the whole purpose is to sensitize yourself to the right mixture. The personal aggregate, which is highly idiosyncratic—the personal mixture that you create out of these various determinants that you may choose from—that is ultimately what you need to develop. And no dietary plan, no stress program plan, no guru, no single form of exercise, is in fact going to resolve that problem.

You can limit the parameters. For instance, if a person wants to exercise, you can tell them that they should do it three times a week on nonconsecutive days for so many minutes, and attain a target pulse protocol, etcetera, etcetera. So you can define the realm of experimentation, but the Aha!, the insight, the adaptation, the infusion of that for the individual, is still a highly private, highly idiosyncratic event. Once the person experiences that, they'll generalize it to other determinants of health and longevity. When you don't see that generalization, then what you have is a devotee. You have a convert, you have a hysterical conversion. You have the person who bores you to tears telling you about *the* latest exercise, or *the* latest guru, or *the* latest meditation technique—all because they have abdicated the eternal quest for self-discovery, for insight, and projected it on some outer authority.

RBA: *This takes us into your most recent book,* Healthy People in Unhealthy Places. *There you focus on the problem of psychophysiological well-being in the workplace, implying that if a concerned individual were truly going to do something about psychophysiologic well-being—in the book you've labeled it optimum health—they would have to revise their whole idea of the workplace and their traditional attitude towards work, because work is where most of life is spent. Is this concentration on the workplace that important?*

Pelletier: The workplace always has been important, and will be more important in the future. One of the fundamental outcomes of a particular historical way of thinking during the Industrial Revolution was that people became interchangeable parts. Just like the parts on an assembly line, people became interchangeable, therefore disposable and replaceable. At present, there is a fundamental shift in the European nations, the United States, and Japan away from heavy manufacturing and the provision of goods, away from the manufacture of steel, even away from the manufacturing of automobiles, toward the provision of services and information management. This implies a greater dependence on the capacity of individuals to learn and develop and move in an organization so that they can provide better human services.

RBA: *And, hopefully, feel secure in that organization.*

Pelletier: And feel secure. Also, we're moving toward a much more information-based society. Information is not a hard product. It's a soft product. It's dependent on the people who deliver it, and to that extent, the individuals involved in the corporate structures are becoming more, not less, important. This concern would be simply a humanistic concern, if it were not for one extremely important factor, which is that up until about five years ago the dollar cost of allowing individuals to become sick, disabled, injured, or even to die as a result of their occupation, was negligible. It really was a small part of the total cost of manufacturing any product or any service. Suddenly, in the past five years, with the unprecedented escalation in the cost of medical care, that relatively insignificant amount of dollars has become a major cost issue. It results in an increase in the cost of manufacturing any given product. General Motors has indicated that it adds over $200 to the cost of an automobile. Chrysler says that they have to manufacture and sell 77,000 automobiles to meet their medical costs in 1984. If you look at current inflation running 5 to 8 percent a year, you find that the inflation of medical costs in this same year runs 20 to 25 percent. Any company has to look at the fact that if they want to remain competitive, then a major factor in reducing costs, which is an obvious part of competition, is how well they can contain these excessive, escalating medical costs. Therefore, for both economic and humanitarian reasons, you need healthy people in healthy places. Those two forces are driving this concern about the individual worker, the collective work force, and the work environment in a way that has never happened since the Industrial Revolution. And it's going to escalate rapidly.

RBA: *Well, that sounds very golden, but let's examine that just a bit. If the workplace is so important, then the employer or, to many, the corporation gains even more ascendancy over the individual and over society. Critics have charged that corporate interest in health is due solely to the corporate motive of reducing costs, and not promoting individual good. Obviously, in mny ways it's all to the individual's good. Yet doesn't this trend give the corporation even greater control than, say, the government here in the United States, over this problem of health and health insurance? Consequently, won't the corporation be doing just as much, maybe more, in creating the medical model that delivers our health care?*

Pelletier: That's a legitimate concern but, I think, an unfounded fear. Unfounded because there are virtually no mandatory health or medical programs in any corporation that I have researched. In fact, of the ones where I have consulted in the development of these programs, there were none. There are certain companies that do have mandatory aspects of medical or health programs, but they are relatively few in number, and they've not been appreciably more effective either in improving the health of their employees or in influencing medical costs than those that are purely voluntary.

That's one point. But a second and probably more important point is that there is a controversial tack being taken in the restructuring of co-payment plans. That is to require workers to pay for a greater and greater share of either their insurance or their care if they become ill. In other words, instead of having first-dollar coverage, deductibles are increased; consequently, the amount of money a worker has to put out before the medical coverage kicks in is higher. Some analysts have objected that this is leaving individuals to their own recourse. But rather than diminishing individual responsibility, it enhances it. It says if you choose to be fifty pounds overweight, to smoke, to eat poorly, and to work under excessive amounts of stress—which in fact may have nothing to do with the workplace—then you are going to have to pay a higher premium to run a higher risk than someone who does not smoke, loses weight, tries to learn something about stress management. We're not talking about pulling the rug out from under an individual worker and saying, okay, now you're on your own, take care of all your medical expenses. We are really talking about voluntary, informed, responsible involvement on the part of individual workers in a seriously conscientious company.

Now the cynic would respond that the company is simply doing that to exploit the worker. And there could be an element of that. But I've studied over 200 of these programs, and there is genuine altruistic concern. Many of the programs were initiated before there were any data to indicate efficacy or return on the investment. They did begin initially with senior executives, but that's sort of obvious since spending dollars to preserve the health of a key executive is more readily justifiable. There are many programs that began with senior executives. Now they've tended to involve larger numbers of the worker base. The point is that these companies that are in the vanguard—IBM, Johnson & Johnson, Xerox, Kimberly-Clark, Bank of America, General Dynamics—these companies have always been in vanguard positions, vis-à-vis manufacturing, training programs for their workers—

RBA: *—and vis-à-vis profits.*

Pelletier: Vis-à-vis profits, and also in the health promotion area. There are also smaller, but *equally effective* programs at the Scherer Brothers Lumber Company and the Mendocino County School District, both of which have received national attention and are being replicated. The point is these are not paternalistic, invasive, manipulative organizations, and I don't think that's going to be the case in the future. But individuals will still be left with the *choice* to be involved or not. If they choose not to be involved, there's no question about the fact that economically and medically they're going to pay a higher price.

RBA: *But isn't this the kind of control that creates a certain kind of material medical model, a highly defined medical model that might keep the general public uninformed of alternatives such as homeopathy or spiritual renewal? One time Mad Bear, the American Indian medicine man, talked about his belief that cancer is a spiritual disease. He offered as evidence the fact that some of the most impressive remissions of cancer come from faith and visualizations, or faith in visualizations. This comes to mind when medical models, or the organized delivery of health care, are considered. In a truly ideal medical model, shouldn't alternative healers be allowed access to insurance coverage, and couldn't corporations lead the way to this? Obviously, politically, the government can't, or won't.*

Pelletier: Let me dissect that. The biomedical model refers essentially to pharmaceuticals, hospitalization, and surgery. That is the Western, allopathic, biomedical model.

RBA: *Yes, very much favoring strict pathology.*

Pelletier: It deals virtually entirely with the diagnosis and treatment of disease per se. That's the definition of medicine according to licensure. It is both a particular and limited diagnostic method, and a particular treatment model. It's not the only model, but when we talk about the biomedical model, that's in general what we're referring to. Now, if you watch what has happened in time, most individuals in Western culture will begin by looking toward the biomedical model to establish and improve their health status. If that fails, is inadequate or incomplete, or simply leaves something wanting, they will then try other practices that involve them more in their own health promotion. This is not within the traditional allopathic model per se. Then we see practices such as medical self-care, nutrition, exercise, meditation, stress management, clinical ecology, social support systems—

the intangible, self-initiated or group-oriented kinds of active involvements on the part of the individual. These are not really in the traditional biomedical model.

We have phrases that have been coined—the biopsychosocial biomedical model, medical self-care, holistic medicine, and behavioral medicine—to describe the integration of things individuals can do for themselves, services that medicine can provide for them, and the interaction between the two. There's also a third category, which are those aspects of health care that fall outside of both of those realms, in the realm of the unproven, the untested—at least within Western tradition—the unknown. These would include approaches such as homeopathy, acupuncture, fasting, various forms of bodywork, certain forms of psychological and psychotherapeutic interventions. Historically you see that people who have tried the second, things they can do for themselves, will also tend to entertain the possibility that approaches in the third category such as homeopathy might be of some help, when in fact these other approaches have not been efficacious.

If we look toward a model ten years from now, it's becoming increasingly clear that the pure allopathic model is too limited, too expensive, is relatively ineffective in chronic, noninfectious diseases such as coronary heart disease, and serves too few people at too high a cost. These are increasingly common kinds of observations found in mainstream publications such as *Science, JAMA,* and the *New England Journal of Medicine.* So we are beginning to realize that we need a new model called behavioral medicine, where medicine does what in fact it can, and the individual does in fact what he or she can. I really do think that other non-Western models will begin to be assessed—they already are. Some, such as acupuncture for certain forms of chronic pain, have been tested, proved out, if you will, much the same way that we've explored other areas. Perhaps in the future these will include further innovations in acupuncture, homeopathy, and some of other methods not commonly used right now.

RBA: *Yet shouldn't we be talking about the individual freedom of bringing health care down to something practical? If the individual is responsible for well-being, shouldn't or couldn't that individual be free to use the medical model for alternative care if she or he so decides? Do you think the corporate health program should entertain, or allow, this kind of freedom?*

Pelletier: Well, actually the problem is that it's not within the province of the corporation to decide what is considered legitimate, and therefore reimbursible. The person with their own money and their own time is free to do whatever they wish. But when you ask the question: is this something that I can go and have done and have reimbursed, that's really a question for the insurance carrier— already one step removed from the corporation. At the present time, the corporation cannot mandate that decision one way or the other. They could influence that process by influencing the third-party or insurance carriers. This is in fact taking place. Blue Cross, Equitable, Allstate, and Metropolitan are presently examining programs such as the behavioral management of hypertension, effective smoking cessation, stress management programs, and optimal nutrition menus—to name but a few examples. Is it more cost effective for the insurance company and the corporation to manage hypertension behaviorally than simply to leave high blood pressure untreated until it results in a heart attack or other kinds of complications? Corporations and government research programs are beginning to look seriously at such questions. Now, you need to remember that the behavioral management of hypertension—from the perspective of the traditional, strictly defined biomedical model—is terribly innovative, unproven, and suspect. The point is that what I look at is the trajectory or the trend behind this, and I've found a definite movement on the part of the carriers that makes it increasingly likely that people will be able to seek out alternative approaches and have them reimbursed. In fact, our Division of Internal Medicine is currently carrying out a three-year research project funded by the U.S. Department of Health and Human Services. The project is based on a request for proposals that indicated a growing concern that more and more of the postwar baby boom are growing older and will be on anti-hypertensive medications for longer periods of time. Among the consequences of long-term use of even the "safe" anti-hypertensives are depression, sexual dysfunction including impotence for men, memory loss, and other psychological impairments. So we are comparing three groups—those on medication only, behavioral intervention only, and behavioral plus medication interventions. We will see a great deal more research as both consumers and researchers realize *pills are not panaceas.*

There are, however, ironic complications. Right now, today, in the Senate, a bill is about to be introduced by Representative Claude Pepper that would essentially outlaw all so-called "unproven therapeutic interventions." The standards that would be used to judge whether something was proven or unproven would be standards set by the allopathic, biomedical model. It would even exclude that middle ground that we call behavioral-medical, and would certainly exclude experimentation or systematic inquiry into the whole area of alternative interventions. That bill is likely to be more important than what the corporations, individuals, or insurance companies do. Actually, the bill was written to protect senior citizens from quackery and exploitation, which is rampant and has to be stopped. However, costly and excessive exploitation occurs in *both* allopathic and alternative practices. The Department of Health and Human Services has statistics indicating 1.7 million unnecessary surgeries in 1983, and there have been complications from ostensibly safe and proven drugs such as thalidomide and procedures such as irradiation of the thyroid. There is no need to belabor these abuses, except to point out that abusive practices are not confined to one approach to health care. We need to clean house across the board.

RBA: *Congressional efforts to bar "unproven practices" may have a greater impact than the efforts of insurance companies or corporations to protect the public's health. On the other hand, we may be getting into an area where the critic can cry corporate apology! The corporation all of a sudden stands aside and says, it's up to the insurance company, or look what's going on in Congress, when in America in 1980, certainly 1990, the corporation is not only growing in power, but is more politically powerful than most people care to admit. How much can the corporation determine? If I'm in a corporation, and responsible for my health, shouldn't I be free to choose alternative care, and shouldn't that care be paid for by health care plans in which I am responsible for my health or well-being?*

Pelletier: My personal opinion is yes, that should be the case, and there are indications that it will occur. In California there has been a movement toward what is termed licensure by disclosure. At the present time, certain degrees allow you to be licensed to practice within certain specialties. This is the traditional model, in which an outside governing board stipulates what you can and cannot do, what you can and cannot state about yourself, what you can and cannot do with a patient. Licensure by disclosure is a quite different model. It simply says that when a person comes to you, you are required to give full disclosure about your background—what you're capable of doing and what your claims are—and on that basis, the person enters into a contractual relationship with you, a relationship of informed consent. What this does is it simply opens up the entire realm of both orthodox and unorthodox practice.

Now whether or not this will be reimbursed by an insurance carrier is another matter altogether, but at least the precedent for acknowledging that there are legitimate alternative methods is established.

Secondly—and this is of concern to insurance companies—I hope I did not give the impression that the insurance companies or the government hold ultimate sway. We like to think in terms of black and white—x causes y, or x is where the power resides, and it causes y. That is not the way things occur. One example: there are a number of corporations that in the face of rising medical insurance costs have refused to pay for the traditional system and have become partially or totally self-insured. What they then do is take the money they would pay to a major insurance carrier and set up their own clinics, their own biomedical-model care clinics and HMOs. Some of these have been the ones that have been most innovative about behavioral medicine.

So insurance companies now have a bellwether, which some such as Blue Cross and Metropolitan have recognized. They realize there is not an infinite escalation they can make in their costs, because at some point the corporations who are their subscribers are going to go elsewhere or are going to establish their own programs. In a case where a corporation has set up its own program, it's entirely capable of saying yes, we will honor whatever forms of alternative methods will save the corporation time and money, keep people healthy and on the job, and not cost an excessive amount. This revision may very well govern a great deal of what we see in health care over the next decade.

RBA: *It may also change the shape of the biomedical model. Many feel that model needs to be reshaped. It has some serious problems, and the principal problem seems to be one of ethics. Could you go into that?*

Pelletier: Yes, but let me make one observation at this point. There is a widespread and growing realization that medicine is not synonymous with health—that the biomedical model is not synonymous with either individual, cultural or historical health. That old misconception lies at the root of a tremendous amount of confusion. Let me cite an example of what I mean. In 1974, Franz Ingelfinger, a physician and, at that time, chief editor of the *New England Journal of Medicine,* stated that "80 percent of conditions" that we see as disease reside *outside* of the province of medical care—that only 10 percent of what we view as disease can be very efficaciously treated by medical technology. These are largely traumatic injuries, clearly diagnosed surgical procedures, obstetrics, and decreasing infant mortality. Ingelfinger then noted that in 10 percent of the cases— due to inadequate diagnosis, iatrogenic or intervention-related problems—the patient actually becomes more incapacitated as a result of medical intervention. His final line was that "therefore the balance of accounts ends up marginally on the positive side of zero." Now, that statement was quite devastating, yet it's as true now, a decade later, as it was then. And the major insight is that the principal determinants of health lie outside the biomedical model.

It's interesting here to look at the research by Thomas McKeown, a conservative British physician, reported in a 1979 book, *The Role of Medicine.* McKeown went back and studied the mortality in major ancient infectious diseases—tuberculosis, pneumonia, scarlet fever, pertussis, and smallpox. He found that every major ancient plague had declined to within 10 percent or less of its high incidence *before* there was any medical intervention. This was due largely to improvements in sanitation, better ventilation, provision of foods (the agrarian revolution still remains the single major factor in improved health), reductions in family size, drainage of swamps, and greater economic equality so that people were able to clothe and feed themselves better. The point being that determinants completely outside of the biomedical model have been, and *will remain,* the major determinants of what is experienced as individual and collective health.

This is even more true now, when we look at the non-infectious diseases—cancer, heart disease, arthritis, respiratory disease, depression, and the whole range of psychological disorders. The major contributing factors to the "afflictions of civilization," the "modern plagues," or the "diseases of indulgence," as one World Health Organization observer once labeled them, are *lifestyle* determinants. We all know the list: stress, diet, exercise, tobacco, alcohol, both prescribed and recreational drugs, and dangerous driving habits. Automobile accidents are the obvious example. This third leading cause of death in the United States was reduced by lower speed limits and seat belts, *not* by more or superior trauma centers. These determinants are largely going to yield to behavioral medical interventions, since they are not adequately addressed by the old biomedical model. That is increasingly evident.

What we need is an ecological model that is both external and internal, something that will give rise to conditions by which we can elicit and sustain health. Now that would be a true health care system, rather than the obvious misnomer we now have. What we don't know at this point is what the shape of the intervention system is going to look like. That's the only thing we don't know. The fact that the old model doesn't work is a certainty.

RBA: *Before going on to immunology, let's touch a little more on intervention. It's obvious the medical model has other problems, and the most glaring one seems to be the problem of medical ethics. That's seen on many levels. Recently, with the flurry of heart transplants, there has been both awe and skepticism regarding the use of surgical intervention in medicine. It has social ramifications that affect the individual, affect medicine, and affect society—infect and effect. In San Francisco, reacting to the heart transplant of Baby Jane Doe, one wag asked, "What's the world's fastest mammal?" The answer was a baboon passing the Loma Linda Hospital, east of Los Angeles. Be that as it may, there are dramatic ethical questions involved. One is whether modern medicine has ceased developing chemotherapeutic and surgical procedures with experimentation on laboratory animals and gone on to experiment on human beings, covering the transition with very expensive, heart-rending publicity campaigns. That's a social question, rising out of a social impression.*

However, concerned individuals know the problems of ethics are of deep concern to almost everyone in the medical community, especially in other areas such as abortion and the right to die. Since most agree it's dangerous to hope to solve ethical considerations politically, what do you feel should be done by those within the medical community, as well as those outside, who realize the gravity of this problem? Shouldn't this problem be brought out more, and shouldn't the concerned speak out on this, from both within and without the medical community?

Pelletier: Of course. Just as the determinants of health reside largely outside the province of medicine per se, the resolutions to the problems of medical and biological ethics are only partially resolvable by answering the medical questions per se. It may, in fact, be on the order of only another 10 percent. The reality is that physicians want their patients to live. The death of a patient is seen as both a personal and a professional failure. There's no question about that, and it's always heart-rending. When a patient dies, it is emotionally trying to the physician who's been caring for that person. There are no ifs, ands, or buts about that, no matter how much professional detachment takes place. But there also is the reality that many times, whenever people are faced with these kinds of life-and-death decisions, the family or others around the individual patient abdicate responsibility. They really don't want to be involved. They want somebody else to take charge. They want somebody else to say yes or no. They want someone else to say, is this person alive? Do we or do we not take them off the resuscitation unit? Is this person beyond hope or not? In other words, they would like not to discuss that possibility because, perhaps, they are even more afraid of death, and the implications of the death of that person, and their own death, than the attending physician.

RBA: *And so it falls on the physician, as not only an ethical problem but a legal problem.*

Pelletier: Precisely. So if you were to construct a board of arbitration, you would unquestionably have physicians, lay people, ministers, philosophers, lawyers, psychologists, and social workers. It's an issue of life and death, and that's an eternal question—a concern for every person in every culture, every profession, throughout time. It's not a medical issue, although it's been medicalized, because now death mostly occurs in a hospital ward. As an example: because of the extraordinary resuscitation methods that are now available, it has become so problematic to determine the fine line between life and death that some hospitals have actually instituted a chart entry called DNR, or Do Not Resuscitate orders. There's an explicit procedure by which the physician engages the family and writes in the progress reports, essentially, "Do not resuscitate"—do not take heroic measures to keep this individual alive. This is a procedure that requires the involvement of the family, requires the involvement of the physician, and I think eventually will perhaps require the involvement of a spiritual counselor in the process. That's the level of concern we're faced with.

Another side to the bioethics of death is that there are now very, very good data about survival rates after heroic procedures are performed on people in hospitals. The reality is that after those heroic procedures are performed, at enormous cost dollarwise, at devastating psychological and personal cost to the family, at cost to the patient—and often to the physician—the survival rate is extremely low. Now we know that, and those statistics are absolutely mind-boggling, because they ask: is it worth it? Yet deciding how much a life is worth is not a question that can be answered in the biomedical model per se. That's in the realm of ethics, spiritual beliefs, social and cultural mores, and the family's wishes. It involves the spiritual realm and spiritual concerns. So, if you take those two examples—how do you decide to note Do Not Resuscitate, and can we in fact keep paying more and more to keep individuals alive when, in fact, we're getting very little quality or quantity of survival for those dollars—how is that weighed? Those are profound concerns.

Another whole realm is with artificial organ implants. Who are the recipients? With the costs of organ transplants and prosthetic devices going higher and higher, the question becomes: who is going to be eligible? Is it only the person who has enough money to afford it? Is there going to be any hope for individuals who don't have enough money to pay for it themselves, to even be eligible for, say, a coronary bypass? Again, these are ethical questions.

Now, the reality is that medical care has always been rationed. There have always been a limited number of people who have had access to the best of care. The modern illusion that we have fostered is that it's accessible to everyone. It's not. It really never has been, except in the few sterling instances you can point to of the very poor individual who happened to get the best possible medical care for a specific condition. Those days are numbered, because insurance companies, MediCal, and Medicare simply cannot afford to provide the best possible medical care for all individuals. So, who is going to get it? Again—ethical considerations. And again, 90 percent of the resolution is going to lie outside of the medical care system. Many physicians would not want to participate in these decisions. They would rather be left to practice what they do best, which is medicine, than be involved in such matters. Still, they need and want other people to get involved.

RBA: *Well, the real point is that ethics has to be brought out of the medical community and brought into the nation at large.*

Pelletier: No question. As much in medicine as in nuclear war or in the preserving of the environment. The resolution of such issues will involve the full range of ethics, the full range of responsibility, in order to address the fundamental significance of any of these questions. Medicine is simply symptomatic of a tendency we have to abdicate responsibility, to shirk issues of ethics, of moral, individual, and cultural responsibility. It's pervasive and corrosive.

RBA: *In other words, just as peace can't be left to the military, the larger questions of life can't be left to the physician.*

Pelletier: I agree 100 percent.

RBA: *So, let's move along to psychoneuroimmunology. One of the reasons we've wanted to talk about it is that in a conversation several months ago you spoke about psychoimmunology and we began investigating it, but found that it wasn't simply psychoimmunology. It was psychoneuroimmunology—or it was neuropsychoimmunology. No matter; what is it? And why does the biologist seem to want to capture it as well? Isn't that deterministic?*

Pelletier: Actually, the field has many names, but the one that will probably stick is psychoneuroimmunology. It was given that name by virtue of being the title of the first definitive compendium of articles about the field, edited and compiled by Robert Ader, of the University of Rochester in New York—the 1981 book, *Psychoneuroimmunology.*

Basically, if you break it down, it's really a simple statement. "Psycho" is consciousness, the mind; "neuro" is the brain and the central nervous system; and "immunology" is by and large the body's biochemistry—in particular, the immunological system. The basic function of the immune system is to differentiate "self" from "non-self." A virus, a bacterium, anything that is foreign to the self is identified by the immune system and, in fact, eliminated. That's external vigilance. Equally important, the immune system provides internal vigilance, which also recognizes self, meaning appropriate cells, from non-self in the form of inappropriate cells or potential malignancies. So when a cell divides abnormally—the current theories of cancer are that we all have potentially malignant cells, and even subclinical cell masses, at any given time—our immune system oversees that division and destroys those cells; in fact, eliminates them. These functions are performed by T cells for cell-mediated immunity and B cells for humoral immunity, as well as by natural killer cells and macrophages, or large scavenger cells, in a complex and as yet poorly understood *system* of interaction that is inherently holistic. So, the basic function of the immune system is to maintain the integrity of our entire organism.

Now, there have been sporadic research findings going back almost fifty years that have suggested that the immune system can be conditioned; in other words, behaviorally influenced. There are reports of asthmatic patients who sneeze at photos or plastic flowers, and of patients who break out in hives under similar conditions. Yet these were largely dismissed, because the immune system was thought to be an autonomous biological system, not influenceable by the mind. The particular series of experiments performed by Robert Ader and the immunologist Nicholas Cohen were very elegant and very simple in their findings. What they did, in essence, was to manipulate the rats' love of saccharin water. Ader and Cohen wanted to see if they could counter-condition the rats to be averse to saccharin water. They used a drug that induced temporary gastrointestinal upset and nausea, and added that to the saccharin-flavored water. What happened was that the rats developed an aversion to the saccharin water because it would give them an intestinal upset. When those same rats were encouraged to drink saccharin-flavored water, which in fact was not accompanied by the drug, they noticed that a number of the rats died due to complications secondary to the suppression of their immune system.

This surprised them. Why would a rat die from drinking a favorite thing, saccharin-flavored water? They asked an immunologist why this occurred, and what they found was that cyclophosphamide, the initial drug given to the rats, was an immunosuppressing drug. Therefore when those rats began drinking the saccharin, they had associated immune suppression with the taste of the saccharin. Even without the drug they were behaviorly suppressing the immunological system. That was a very significant finding. Ader and Cohen's basic experiment has been replicated with many variations and subtleties since. Essentially, what it points to is the fact that the immune system can in fact be conditioned via psychological processes to be suppressed. The question is, can it also be enhanced?

At the human level, there was another research project conducted at Mount Sinai by Marvin Stein and his associates. This looked at a number of husbands of wives who were dying of breast cancer. They followed the immunological status of these husbands up to and after the death of their wives. What they found was that the husbands' immunological systems were compromised or suppressed. In other words, the number and activity of certain cells in the immune system were decreased—acutely—for from two to four months after the death of the spouse—and for upwards of a year in some individuals. So these husbands would be predisposed to viral/bacterial infection and also potentially would be more predisposed to cancer through the unchecked development of subclinical malignancy. This demonstrated that in human beings depression, fear, and sorrow do have a profound effect on the immunological system, and that effect lasts for a period of time.

Another point here—there is a rather large body of literature that demonstrates that acute stress can have an immune-*enhancing* effect. So when we have a short-term injury—a cut, a bruise, or a short-term stress—the immune system is actually enhanced. There's also other research that shows that chronic stress, because of the influence of other chemicals in the body—adrenaline, catecholamines, corticosteroids, and other stress-related hormones—has the effect of decreasing the immunological function. So you could think about chronic stress predisposing a person to developing, or being susceptible to, those things over which the immune system normally maintains vigilance.

It's a very promising area. To me, if you look at this area, it has the same kind of tentative information, lacking a basic model, that characterized the field of cell biology prior to the discovery of the structure of DNA in the early 1950s. It is a field waiting for a Watson-and-Crick model to define more clearly how mental processes are translated—both by the central nervous system and by the body's biochemistry—into either an end organ disease or state of health.

One last thing—if you look back historically in the area of psychopysiology, or mind/body, mind/brain interaction, you find that up until about the mid-1950s we had essentially an electrical model. We were measuring the electricity of the brain and the central nervous system, and trying to theorize about how mind and the electrical system could interact to account for certain states of disease or health. Hans Selye's great innovation was the monitoring of the adrenocorticotrophic hormones, or ACTH. What Selye did was demonstrate that you could relatively simply measure a biochemical variable that in turn gave you another level of explanatory power. You could then say, Aha! Now here we have a whole set of blood chemistries that we can measure, that we can use to explain how mind and body interact. That spawned another generation of both theory and practical application about the psychophysiology of health and disease. To me, the past five years—these real breakthroughs right on the edge of psychoneuroimmunology—mark a third stage. Now, when you bring the immune system into play, the explanatory power on a theoretical basis and thus the clinical potential and clinical applications are again given a quantum leap in terms of being able to explain this subtle mind/body, mind/immune system interaction.

There are other promising findings, such as *direct* central nervous system pathways via the hypothalamus to the pituitary, so the nervous system and immune system are directly linked. Also, both the nervous system and the immune system share the same "words" or "vocabulary" of communication, in the form of shared neuropeptides.

There are other important findings from recent studies in multiple personalities (as in the classic movies *The Three Faces of Eve* and *Sybil*), where one personality is a diabetic and the other is not, but both are in the same body! At the National Institute of Mental Health, psychiatrist Frank Putnam has found that the EEGs, or brain wave records, of the split personalities are as different from each other as between two different people. There may be as many as twenty personalities, with twenty different mind/body patterns, in one sea of body chemistry. Unraveling this will not be easy, but this is characteristic of breakthrough areas.

RBA: *So, in a sense, translated down again to our lone concerned individual out there, trying to live a larger life, what this means, in effect, is that the power of thought can actually bolster or improve the immune system.*

Pelletier: Yes. It is a definite influence.

RBA: *And this of course would lead to greater individual control over optimum health. But wouldn't the practice of meditation be a definite advantage then? If an individual can send out thoughts to improve her or his immune system, wouldn't the practice of meditation be the perfect vehicle? Wouldn't it be a great advantage to transport this thought?*

Pelletier: Let me frame that, and then answer it. If we look out over the next decade, perhaps two decades, we realize that the mind/body system is set up in such a way that it is modifiable and as susceptible to very subtle influences as it is to gross, macrocosmic influences. The question is not: do you have a big enough key to unlock the door? The question is: what is the right key, the right size, the right combination? Subtle energies *can* influence health. Belief systems influence health. Social support systems influence health. The existence of non-ionizing, electromagnetic radiation—seemingly innocuous radiation from television transmitters or microwave emissions used in communications—these, in fact, have influences on biological systems. These can be negative and disruptive to cells or they can be positive in the potential to regenerate cells, bone—perhaps entire organs! The point is that we will develop a model of mind/body interaction and subsequent clinical interventions that deal better with subtle energies, that actually influence the outcome.

Now, in this category you could include providing adequate shielding or controls for exposure to non-ionizing electromagnetic radiation. We could recognize that the antibiotics fed to beef and chickens in fact produce strains of resistant bacteria affecting the human species that are not responsive to normal levels of antibiotics. Also, we may come to recognize that subtle levels of pollution in the environment produce birth defects and high infant mortality, or—twenty or thirty years later—cancers not detectable on a shorter-term basis. In other words, subtle influences may in fact be governing much of what we perceive as health or the lack of health.

Within that category, I would add that meditation is clearly one of the most important disciplines that an individual can undertake. It has both mental and physical benefits and, also, out of such practice grows a certain sensitivity, an orientation, a certain degree of insight into self and others and the world as a whole, which is more compassionate, more embracing—more cognizant of systems and how systems interact and affect each other. When one has an inkling of that perspective, one is less likely to act in either a personally, environmentally, or globally destructive way. Meditation is absolutely not to be confused with a particular sect, a particular person, or a particular belief. That's not what meditation is. It is a generic form of practiced, disciplined insight into the nature and structure of the human mind, devoid of a particular guru or method. A person may choose a ·method, but it's not the same as the practice of meditation per se.

RBA: *It's no different than having a brand name.*

Pelletier: Exactly.

RBA: *Idealistically then, in the future, can we hope that psycho-neuroimmunology, which sounds so exciting, won't fall into the deterministic hands of the biologists or the devotees of chemotherapeutic intervention? Can we hope that psychoneuroimmunology* *will provide individual power, and an individual advantage in the coming century—one that would be less scientifically oriented, less religiously controlled?*

Pelletier: Clearly the greatest influence in the area of psycho-neuroimmunology is being exerted by the traditional biologists and immunologists. If you look at the equation, it's rather lopsided. The immunology is overemphasized. The neuro is rather marginal, but there is some promising evidence about direct neurological inner-vation of the endocrine/immunological system. In other words, there is a direct connection between the central nervous system and the immune system. The connection to the psycho or consciousness dimension is extremely distant in the minds of the biologist and the immunologist. That balance needs to be redressed. Right now, however, major texts still treat the immunological system as an autonomous system devoid of psychoneurological influence. I believe that will change.

For instance, if you look at AIDS as an example of a psycho-neuroimmunological disease, most of the ongoing research projects are essentially looking at it in terms of biological immunological process. However, a few projects presently funded by the U.S. Department of Health and Human Services are looking at the fact that certain lifestyle predispositions—largely characterized by de-pression, by excessive antibiotic consumption, by having had a long history of opportunistic diseases prior to the onset of the AIDS syndrome—all of these predisposing factors may set the person up for AIDS. Now, after a person has AIDS, then the pure biomedical methods may in fact be more appropriate. But if we consider how we prevent its occurrence in the first place, then we have to start looking at the behavioral end of the equation. That's the balance we need in a true model of behavioral or holistic medicine.

It's always easier, and scientists always feel more comfortable, when you come down with both feet on one side of the equation. You've got the support of your peers and of your colleagues. If immunologists cross the line, they get resistance from their col-leagues, as well as resistance from the field they're entering. And if a psychologist crosses the line to neurology or immunology, you get the censure of your peers, you get the resistance of the field you're trying to enter. And they are very formidable. There's no ifs, ands, or buts about that. So, those are the forces mitigating against the larger view. But, more and more, if you look at the literature you find that researchers and publications are crossing lines. This is in the mainstream reports of scientific literature.

RBA: *It was interesting to see, in a recent issue of the bulletin of the Institute of Noetic Sciences, that they talked about this whole area. It seems that the mind/body discipline that you've been talking about as psychoneuroimmunology has splintered off into a number of other disciplines, depending, of course, on where you started. There is now something called Positive Emotions Research. That's apparently where the Simonton work in cancer therapy, for example, gets pigeonholed. It seems really critical that people in these different areas begin talking to one another. How can that be encouraged?*

Pelletier: Well, actually, Robert Ader was able to capture the essence of the field called psychoneuroimmunology in approximately sixty articles, and so for a brief moment he had, by and large, captured the field. Now, suddenly, there's an avalanche of research activity in a field that looks so promising. What tends to happen because of the plethora of articles and data that flows out of this is that instead of trying to maintain a composite or a collective overview of the field, individual researchers tend to retreat back into their own discipline and area of expertise. Of course, there are two reasons for this. One is personal—because they feel this way they can maintain efficacy, credibility, and precision. The second is even more practical: unless you do that, you do not get funded for highly speculative research, because any research proposal is reviewed by a panel of peers, and inherently a panel of peers tends to be conservative.

RBA: *This is the curse of specialization.*

Pelletier: Exactly, and it gets reinforced. In other words, the natural predisposition encouraged in science, one of caution and conservatism, is reinforced by the collective pressure of limited peer review. So those who know for certain they can conduct a limited, small-scale, highly focused research project and get it funded will do so—because they have mortgages, children in school, a spouse who wants a new car, or they want a vacation, or whatever.

RBA: *And they have a laboratory staff to keep going.*

Pelletier: They have a laboratory staff to keep going. So they have both personal and professional predisposing factors. Now, that's the negative side. On the positive side there's the Institute for the Advancement of Health, which is now two years old, initially established by Eileen Rockefeller. The purpose of the Institute is to integrate these findings and try to maintain a cohesive overview of this emerging field of psychoneuroimmunology and health in general. It does so through its publications, a magazine called *Advances,* and also through annual meetings on the East and West coasts. It brings together people who are doing very basic research in neurosciences and psychoneuroimmunology, and encourages discourse and cross-fertilization.

The ultimate touchstone for science is: does it produce adequate, parsimonious theory that generates experiments that can confirm or disprove theory? That's the touchstone of science. Now, the extent to which collaborative, cross-disciplinary work produces better theory with experimentation that proves or disproves underlying theory—if it can do that better than highly specialized, highly fragmented research—is the key to whether or not it will thrive and become a model of how to conduct science. If it does not, it will fail. And rightfully so. That is what's hanging in the balance.

RBA: *And that's one way to correct schisms, so to speak*

Pelletier: Exactly. And the touchstone will be whether cross-disciplinary collaboration creates a more comprehensive science or not. If it does, it will thrive, and if it doesn't, the specialists will rightfully reign.

Kenneth Pelletier was interviewed by Robert Briggs in Oakland, California, January 3, 1985.

THE REFLEXIVE UNIVERSE by Arthur M. Young
Introduction by Jacob Needleman
Considered by Colin Wilson to be "the most important volume of
cosmology to be published in the past twenty-five years," THE RE-
FLEXIVE UNIVERSE integrates scientific laws with the evolution of
consciousness, disclosing common ground between esoteric thought
and modern science.

293 pages $12.95 Trade Paperback

Order Form

To order: enclose check or money order and mail to:
Robert Briggs Associates
Publishers Services
POB 2510
Novato, California 94948

________ THE REFLEXIVE UNIVERSE
@ $12.95 (paper-6-9) ________

________ BRAIN SCALE OF DR. BRUNLER
@   2.95 (paper-01-7) ________

________ EAST & WEST
@   2.95 (paper-00-9) ________

________ COMMON BOOK OF CONSCIOUSNESS
@   7.95 (paper-3-4) ________

________ DARWINISM
@   2.95 (paper-8-5) ________

________ A NEW AGE
@   3.95 (paper-02-5) ________

Purchase ________

California sales tax 6%

In BART Counties, Santa Clara, Santa Cruz,
San Mateo, & Los Angeles Counties add 6½%   ________

Postage & Handling:
Orders UNDER $6 - add 1.00
Orders OVER $6 - add 2.00   ________

TOTAL AMOUNT ________

☐ CHECK ENCLOSED   ☐ VISA   ☐ MASTER CHARGE

ACCT #: ____

EXP DATE: ______/__________ SIGNATURE:_________________________

SHIP TO:

ADDRESS:

CITY

STATE   ZIP